WEATHER

BRIAN COSGROVE

For Reference

Not to be taken from this room

D1523187

Airlife
England

> *To Shelley*
> *Ever a ray of sunshine*

Copyright © 2002 Brian Cosgrove

First published in the UK in 2002
by Airlife Publishing Ltd

British Library Cataloguing-in-Publication Data
A catalogue record for this book
is available from the British Library

ISBN 1 84037 235 4

Typeset by Echelon, Wimborne
Printed in China

Airlife Publishing Ltd
101 Longden Road, Shrewsbury,
SY3 9EB, England
E-mail: airlife@airlifebooks.com
Website: www.airlifebooks.com

CONTENTS

Introduction	**1**
The Problem	**2**
Opening Up the Subject	**5**
Pressure	**8**
Wind	**14**
Temperature	**19**
Moisture in the Air	**31**
Clouds	**37**
Precipitation	**53**
Air Masses	**60**
Weather	**65**
Frontal Systems	**74**
Weather Reporting	**85**
The Future	**90**
Index	**92**

INTRODUCTION

Weather is the same the world over – it is extremes that vary according to the geographical location on our planet.

You are assumed to have never come across the subject before or to have forgotten what may have been covered in school-days past. The basics will be explained to you and it is possible a reader with some prior knowledge of meteorology may consider many aspects to have been omitted or not fully explained. This is intentional as 'sufficient for the day is the evil thereof'. The full picture can be learned from other books for those who wish to take the next step.

THE PROBLEM

And that is the end of the news; we now go over to the weather centre to see what is in store for us.' Onto the TV screen appears the well-known face of a duty forecaster who presents you with a map. But this map reveals no roads, railways, rivers and suchlike: instead you can be faced with a multitude of lines, sometimes depicting circles and at other times meandering aimlessly in all directions.

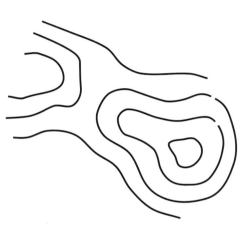

To these lines can be added other lines crossing them; one line may have 'mole hills' (usually red) along the edge, and is normally associated with another line edged with pointed 'triangles' (usually blue).

Frequently the red and blue lines join at the top; from this point a third line can shoot up from the point at which they merge.

Obviously, having been produced by the two previous lines, and in order not to be biased, this line compromises by accepting both 'mole hills' and pointed 'triangles' alternately!

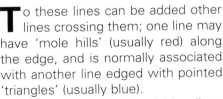

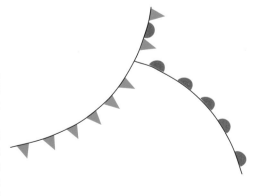

A picture is supposed to speak a thousand words. But in this case it could mean that only the words count: for many of you the map is basically meaningless. At some time or another the puzzled look on your face may be mercifully relieved by the introduction of a variety of identifiable symbols. If the symbols do mean something to you then you are justified in asking – 'Why on earth is the map cluttered with the other jumble?' The truth is that without the mass of lines the forecaster would not be able to produce forecast in the first place. They used to support the reasons for symbols (and perhaps to arouse interest of people like yourself to delve a little deeper).

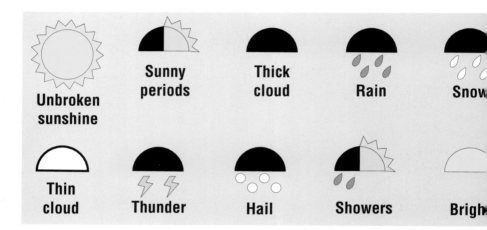

Unbroken sunshine

Sunny periods

Thick cloud

Rain

Snow

Thin cloud

Thunder

Hail

Showers

Brigh

Possible symbols

So why not join in and see what they mean and how they justify any symbols being used. Yes, I know that meteorology is a science and that could be enough to put you off. In fact, you might as well know from the outset that it is also dubbed an inexact science because of the foibles of nature. Having said that, present-day technical progress is such that forecasts are now far more accurate than in the past.

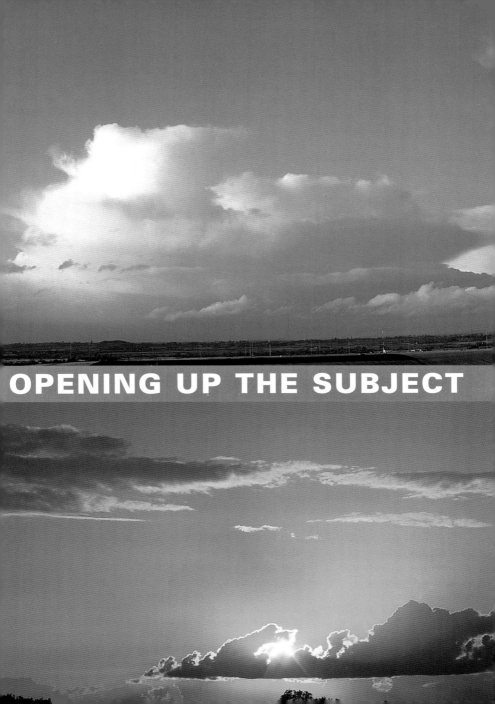

OPENING UP THE SUBJECT

It should not take too much imagination to appreciate that at the Poles it will be cold and at the Equator it will be hot. Naturally the change from south to north or north to south is the gradual one which brings about the seasons. These variations are due to the slant of the earth in relation to the sun according to the time of year and its position. The sun will be over the Equator only twice a year – in March and September. At other times it will appear to be moving north from the Equator after March in order to be over the Tropic of Cancer (Northern Hemisphere) in June, and moving south after September to be over the Tropic of Capricorn (Southern Hemisphere) in December. The period when the sun is over each of the Tropics is mid-summer in the particular hemisphere, at which point it is mid-winter over the other.

Summer regions

Summer
December
Southern hemisphere

Seasonal position
of Earth
related to Sun

Summer
June
Northern hemisphere

From now on in *The Vital Guide to Weather* the word 'met' will suffice for meteorology – in keeping with the intention to abide by the KISS philosophy (Keep It Simple, Stupid!). Scientific terminology and elements will be avoided and there are very few occasions when mathematics is used – limited mostly to the addition and subtraction of single figures! Also, I have tried where possible to make explanations relate to everyday experiences.

Initially we shall briefly consider the theory behind some of the fundamentals you need to know to understand the practical aspects. This means exploring how winds relate to air pressure, together with the source and effect of temperature and moisture in the atmosphere. We will then look at the various cloud formations and how they occur, the cause of rain/sleet and snow, together with the patterns that cause the weather.

Who knows, it is quite possible that you will be one of the many who become fascinated with the sky – no longer treading the pavement with your head down. The last chapter in this book may seem like a 'commercial', but it could be a useful guide for taking that next step. Now down to work. Let's start by putting on the pressure!

Just one of the skies you may see.

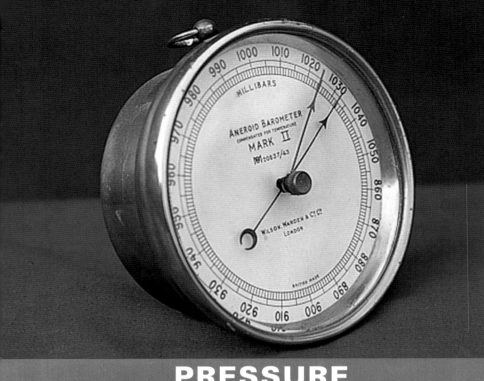

PRESSURE

Pressure is simply the weight of air pressing down on our planet earth. Yes, air does have weight – caused by the force of gravity that keeps its molecules clinging near to the earth's surface instead of drifting into outer space. Naturally the pressure decreases with height until finally reaching outer space where there is simply no more air and therefore no more pressure.

It is important to note that pressure over a given location is constantly changing, hence the terms 'high' one minute and 'low' the next which you can hear during forecasts. To identify where these changes are taking place, measurements have to be taken using a barometer – an instrument no doubt you have seen on the wall of somebody's house if not your own. There are three types.

Aneroid Barometer

This barometer has a drum rather like a concertina and air is sealed within it at a fixed pressure. When outside air is GREATER than the pressure in the drum, the drum is squeezed inwards. This movement is attached to a pointer that indicates on the face of the barometer that the pressure is rising. Similarly, when the pressure outside is LESS than the air contained in the drum, the drum expands and the pointer indicates the pressure is falling.

There is invariably an additional pointer that you can use to mark the pressure reading so that you can readily see if there has been a change or not since the last reading. Also, on the face of the 'domestic-type' barometer you will usually find references to various types of weather. This highlights the direct relationship between pressure and weather.

The aneroid barometer

Mercury Barometer

This barometer consists of a column of mercury with a reservoir at the bottom which contains a tiny hole through which outside air can enter. As outside pressure rises or falls so does the column of mercury which has units of measurement alongside the column. Ornate versions of this type are often seen in antique shops.

The mercury barometer

The barograph

Barograph

This third type of barometer is based on the aneroid principle. Here the pressure value produced by the sealed drum is carried by levers to a revolving chart showing both date and time. The line traced on the chart gives a constant picture of pressure changes as they occur.

The barograph is a very expensive piece of kit which you rarely see in homes these days.

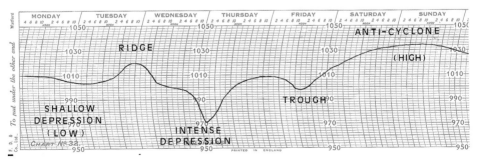

The chart. In official terms a 'low' is called a depression and a 'high' is an anti-cyclone.

Unit of Measurement

The unit of measurement for pressure in most countries was at one time inches, based on the length of the column of mercury in a mercury barometer; in fact the inches term was maintained when the aneroid came into use and it is still used in the United States of America.

In many countries, including Great Britain, the unit that replaced the inch was the millibar (mb) but this has been changed to yet another unit called the hectoPascal (hPa). Since the hPa is of precisely the same value as the millibar one can only assume there is someone (or lots of someones) out there who wishes (in the name of progress) to complicate an otherwise happy situation for we ordinary mortals! As most existing instruments still record in millibars we shall stick to the term for the purposes of this book.

Locating the High and Low Pressure Centres

How can the forecaster tell where those highs and lows are located at a given time? It is now time that we talk about these 'meandering lines' mentioned earlier.

World-wide met observation stations record and report pressure readings at regular intervals every day – together with other aspects of weather. But, as pressure reduces with height, to get a uniform base, all readings from such stations are adjusted to read as if taken at sea level. Finally, lines depicting the millibar (or inch) for the line are drawn on a chart joining all places which have the same pressure; these lines are called isobars.

Pressure patterns from isobars

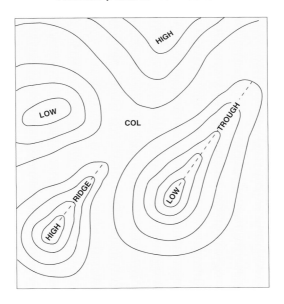

Now we can really begin to see how high and low pressure systems are located, together with two other main terms – the 'ridge' and the 'trough'. These are tongues which can often protrude out of high and low centres respectively. All these systems contribute to forecasting our future weather, as will be discussed later.

The next step is to look into some of the effects that pressure changes can bring about – starting with wind.

Cause of Wind

The period of calm, the gentle breeze, the howling gale and the hurricane all stem from the same source. The cause is the difference in air pressure between locations at any given time. Air behaves like a liquid. Just as water will flow from a full glass if joined to an empty one until reaching the same level in each glass, so air will flow from high pressure to low pressure, aiming to achieve the same balance. Wind is none other than this movement of air.

We need to know two basic things about wind – its speed and its direction. Isobars will provide both answers.

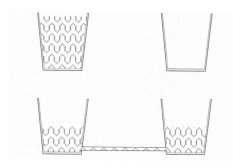

Glasses of water

Wind Direction

t may be a case of 'teaching granny to suck eggs' when telling you how wind direction is reported. It is based on the direction FROM which the wind is blowing with the description derived from the compass, e.g. north, south, south-west, or in degrees related to North for navigational use. It is identified by means of a wind vane.

A change in direction is termed as follows. When it has moved clockwise the wind is said to have veered; when it has moved anti-clockwise it is said to have backed.

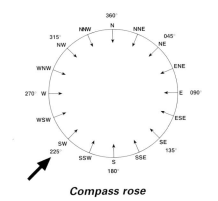

Compass rose

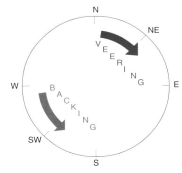

Veering and backing

Wind vanes

Wind Speed

How speed is determined is fairly simple to understand. If you are not still at school, cast your mind back to the days when you were taught about contours on a map; those lines that depict the height of ground above sea level. When the contours are very close together the slope is steep; conversely when they are further apart the slope is shallow. Picture a stream descending down a steep slope; it will be flowing much faster than it would down a shallow slope. So, the sam applies to air when isobars are clos together – the speed from hig pressure to low pressure will be faste

The speed of wind is measured b an anemometer comprised of cup which spin round in the wind.

A specially designed ruler is use for forecasting which, when pu ACROSS the isobars on a forecas chart, will show the approximat expected wind speed.

That wasn't hard was i There is a slight sna however, because you ar quite naturally going t assume from the 'glasses water' example that the pat of the wind will be straigl from high to low. It isn't.

Contours and isobars Mb

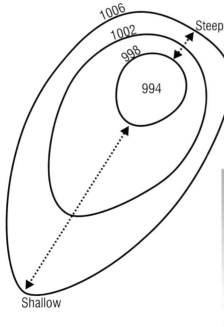

Anemomet

Airflow around a pressure system

Here we come to one of the foibles of met which will be left unexplained due to the earlier promise not to get involved in science. All you need to know is that due to the earth's rotation, instead of blowing directly across the isobars from high to low in an almighty rush, the winds actually blow almost ALONG the isobars near the surface. There is a deflection away from the high towards the low pressure centre around 30 degrees over land and around 10 degrees over the sea. This not only allows the air to flow from high to low, but it also slows the movement from being that almighty rush!

In the Northern Hemisphere the flow around a high pressure centre is always in a clockwise direction and anti-clockwise around a low centre. Once in the Southern Hemisphere the situation becomes reversed. The flow is now anti-clockwise around a high and clockwise around a low. Don't lose sleep by asking why at this stage – it's always been that way.

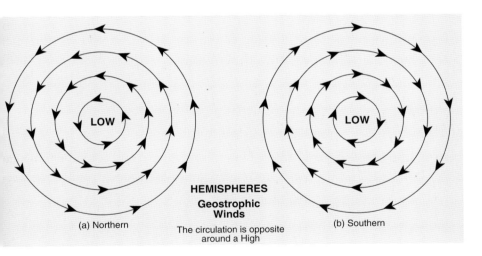

(a) Northern

HEMISPHERES
Geostrophic Winds
The circulation is opposite around a High

(b) Southern

Flow related to isobars around a 'low' in both Northern and Southern Hemispheres. At the Earth's surface the arrows tilt inwards into a 'low' and outwards from a 'high'.

The important points to remember are:

– *Pressure is measured in millibars (mb) but you may hear the word hectoPascal (hPa) used at times and maybe more so in the future. In the USA measurement is still in inches at present.*

– *Isobars joining places of the same sea level pressure produce a picture of pressure systems.*

– *The closer the isobars, the stronger the wind.*

– *Wind flows almost along isobars near the surface – not directly across them with a deflection towards the low pressure centre and away from the high centre.*

– *Flow in the Northern Hemisphere is clockwise around a high and anti-clockwise around a low.*

– *Flow in the Southern Hemisphere is anti-clockwise around a high and clockwise around a low.*

TEMPERATURE

Measurement

Temperature is a word related to how cold or hot we feel so its meaning should need no explanation in itself; equally, the word thermometer (the instrument used to measure it) should be quite well known. In many countries the unit of measurement for heat was for years stated in degrees Fahrenheit (°F) and this unit is still used in the United States which once again seems to have stuck to tradition. In the United Kingdom and many countries it changed to degrees Centigrade and now it is degrees Celsius (°C). (No, I don't know what it will be next!)

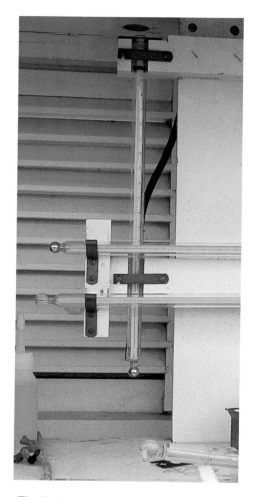

The basic thermometer is the vertical one

So, 0°C, which is the freezing point of water, is 32°F and 100°C, which is the boiling point of water, is 212°F. The method of converting degrees Celsius to degrees Fahrenheit and vice versa requires some mathematics which I promised to keep away from in this book as much as possible. However, for those who revel in multiplication, addition and subtraction, here goes.

Celsius to Fahrenheit is:

C divided by 5, multiplied by 9, plus 32

e.g.
10°C = 10 ÷ 5 = 2
      x 9 = 18
      + 32 = 50°F

Fahrenheit to Celsius is:

F minus 32, divided by 9, multiplied by 5

e.g.
50°F = 50 − 32 = 18
      ÷ 9 = 2
      x 5 = 10°C

There are a number of things worth knowing about temperature in order to understand some of the steps we will be covering later.

Source of Heat

How do we obtain our heat and retain it each day? Is it directly from the sun? No. If this were the case we would freeze to death every night when the sun had gone down. In fact one night would be enough! Picture a central heating system in your home; the boiler doesn't directly heat your rooms – this is done by the radiators which have been heated by the boiler. So it is with Mother Earth. The sun penetrates the atmosphere and heats our planet's surface which in turn absorbs this heat to become in effect the 'boiler'; the surface then radiates the heat back into the atmosphere. Because of this, when the sun has set we do not freeze during the night but survive due to the heat stored during the day still being radiated.

The night can become progressively cooler until the sun rises next day to replenish the boiler. However, there is a factor which greatly influences the extent of radiation at night – it is cloud. A layer of cloud can act as an insulator that substantially reduces the radiation thus slowing down the loss of heat within the atmosphere below cloud level. Naturally, in reverse, a cloud blanket during the day can reduce the input into the 'boiler' but not to any great extent, as you can experience for yourself when the clouds pass across the sun and place you temporarily in the shade.

If you still have the nagging feeling that the heat comes directly from the sun then climb Mount Everest in a swim suit and let me know how you feel when, or rather if, you get back! This climb emphasises an important point to remember – temperature decreases with height. Some 'know all' might now start leaping about – anxious to point out that this decrease is not always the case. This would be correct on certain occasions but we'll talk about it later.

Back into the sunshine. As I mentioned earlier, during the year the sun appears to move back and forth from the Southern to the Northern Hemisphere and vice versa. The amount of heat radiated obviously depends on the seasons of the year.

With this apparent movement of the sun to and from the Northern and Southern Hemispheres it also becomes lower and higher in the sky according to the season. This results in longer or shorter hours of daylight in summer and winter respectively. In fact over the Poles in mid summer there is virtually no night.

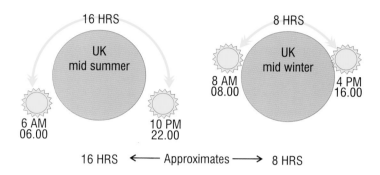

16 HRS

UK
mid summer

6 AM
06.00

10 PM
22.00

8 HRS

UK
mid winter

8 AM
08.00

4 PM
16.00

16 HRS ←—— Approximates ——→ 8 HRS

Mid summer is depicted by the picture at the opening of this chapter. Naturally, when one hemisphere is enjoying summer the other will be suffering the winter.

Earlier it was mentioned that the earth is a 'boiler' which absorbs heat from the sun's rays. The extent to which the heat is absorbed, be it winter or summer, varies according to the nature of the surface that the sun's rays strike. Picture a nice hot summer's day; would you sit on a rock or the grass for your picnic? There should be no prizes for the right answer to that question – unless wearing asbestos underwear, anyone who sits on the rock can expect a rapidly scorched bottom! Conversely, would you prefer to plunge into the sea in April or September? The answer here for anyone but the most hardy would be September. But why?

The rock is one extreme where the hard surface precludes any deep penetration of the sun's rays; thus the full amount of heat received is retained at the surface and is very rapidly noticed. Water is the other extreme where this time the same amount of heat easily penetrates and spreads out to a considerable depth. It therefore takes a long time before the sea in general becomes warmer – in fact the whole summer season is needed to achieve its maximum temperature.

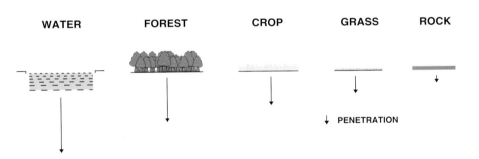

Range of surface heating characteristics

For every event there always seems to be an opposite. At night the hot rock would rapidly emit all the heat concentrated on the surface whereas the water would emit its heat very slowly.

Whilst on this aspect, the diff- erence between the depth to which water can absorb heat compared with land where relatively it is mostly confined to the surface, is best shown by the west coast of America. Note the temperature at the coast compared with that inland.

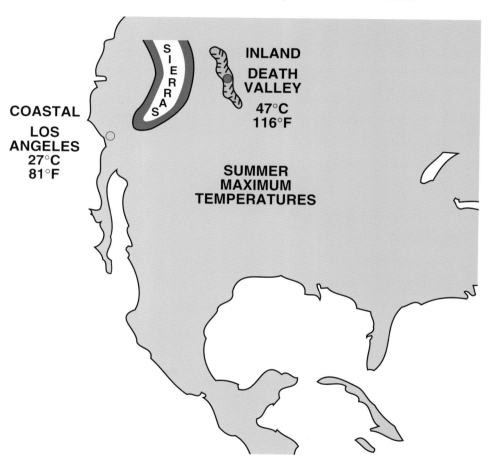

COASTAL LOS ANGELES 27°C 81°F

INLAND DEATH VALLEY 47°C 116°F

SIERRAS

SUMMER MAXIMUM TEMPERATURES

West Coast America and Death Valley

Temperature and the Air

Next we look at the effect of temperature on the air. First, what do you see frequently from a well-lit bonfire in the garden? Embers shoot up from the fire, do they not; but the fire is not a volcano so what makes the embers ascend?

The second example is a hot air balloon with its burner shooting out flames at intervals into the balloon and up it goes – basket, intrepid people and all.

Without delving into the science aspect, suffice it to say that when a 'parcel' of air becomes warmer than its immediate surround (environment), that parcel is forced to rise. The name 'parcel' is used because no one has yet thought of a better name.

You must realise that flames are not necessary to warm the air – going back to the rock and water, a slight change in the surface temperature compared with its surround is sufficient to warm the air in contact with it and make it rise.

You want to know how far up the warm parcel will ascend?

Bonfire with embers shooting up

Hot air balloon leaving the ground

Heat Loss on Ascent

Before understanding the answer to that question there is another aspect of which you should be aware. First, you have been told that the temperature decreases as you climb up through the atmosphere; second, you have been told that a parcel of air decreases in temperature when it is forced to climb up through the atmosphere. It sounds as if the two are the same, does it not? Sadly they behave differently. (I hate having to explain the difference between these two – but here goes.)

In the first situation the temperature decrease with height is a variable in the atmosphere; it will be constantly changing according to the weather conditions at the time. For example, the decrease per 1000 feet at the time could be, say, 4°C (7.2°F) up to 1000 feet of height, 3°C (5.4°F) to 2000 feet, the same *en route* to 3000 feet, with only 2°C (3.6°F) to 4000 feet and so on; the decrease per 1000 feet at any time can vary right to the top of the atmosphere.

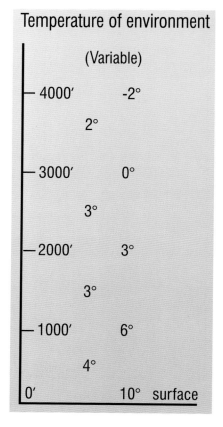

Temperature of environment

(Variable)

| 4000' | -2° |
| 2° |
| 3000' | 0° |
| 3° |
| 2000' | 3° |
| 3° |
| 1000' | 6° |
| 4° |
| 0' | 10° surface |

Varying lapse rates on climb

Temperature of rising air

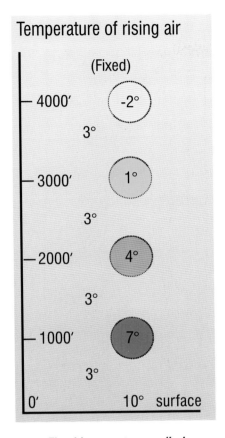

Fixed lapse rates on climb

The second situation concerns the parcel of air being forced to rise up through the variable atmosphere. In this case a parcel of air *forced* to climb through the atmosphere decreases in temperature at a *fixed* rate of ascent of 3°C (5.4°F) per 1000 feet.

Also, the higher its temperature, compared with the environment, the faster the ascent. Here comes your answer as to how far a parcel will climb. It keeps ascending until it reaches a temperature equal to itself; in other words, where the parcel is neither warmer nor cooler than its surround (environment).

Here's yet another 'pearl of wisdom'. A parcel can happen to become cooler than its surround due to an initially fast rate of climb, letting it overshoot the level where it would be equal in temperature. In this case it would immediately slow down, stop, and begin to sink back to the level at which it would be equal in temperature. Just as warm air will rise, cool air will descend.

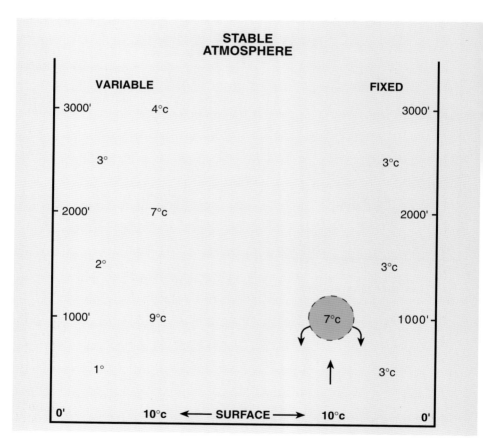

Sinking back to equilibrium – stable conditions

The higher the temperature of a rising parcel relative to its surround, the faster will be the ascent.

At any given time the atmosphere can be said to be in one of two conditions; it is either stable or unstable. These are important atmospheric conditions as they very much influence the types of cloud formation and thereby, the weather. Earlier you saw an example of the parcel very quickly become cooler than its surround and sinking back towards the surface. When it can't climb, the atmosphere is said to be stable. When it keeps climbing conditions are said to be unstable.

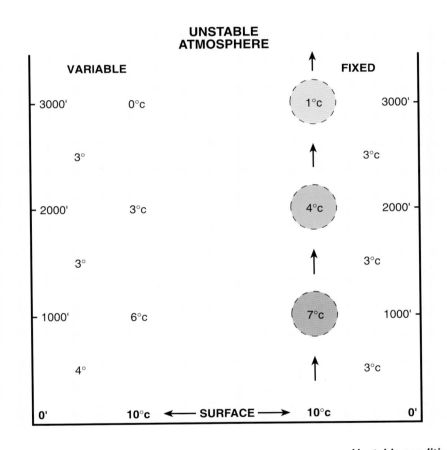

UNSTABLE ATMOSPHERE

Unstable conditions

The important points to remember are:

- The earth radiates warmth into its atmosphere from heat absorbed by the sun.

- Cloud can slow down the loss of heat radiated.

- Temperature decreases with height.

- Uneven surface heating varies according to the nature of the surface.

- The effect of sea on coast compared with inland.

- Air warmer than its surround is FORCED to rise until it cools to the same temperature as the surrounding air.

- Air cooler than its surround will descend until it warms to the same temperature as the surrounding air.

- The decrease in temperature as you climb through the atmosphere can vary.

- A parcel of air forced to climb up through the atmosphere decreases in temperature at the fixed rate of 3°C (5.4°F) per 1000 feet.

- Where a parcel can keep climbing the atmosphere is said to be unstable.

- Where a parcel cannot climb any more, the atmosphere is said to be stable.

MOISTURE IN THE AIR

How many times have you left for work on a cold morning and seen your car covered in water droplets? As there has been no rain, have you not been puzzled on occasions?

Let's see how this comes about and by the way, we are fast approaching the end of the theory side so hang on in there!

Relative Humidity

Air contains invisible water vapour that can vary in its amount. The met term used for assessing the vapour content in a parcel is known as Relative Humidity (RH). Yes, I know that using such a term is getting close to the science aspect but I feel you can live with this one! Quite simply it is the amount of water vapour in a parcel of air at a given time – related to the maximum amount that parcel could hold. So, if the air contains only half the amount of vapour it is able to contain then the RH is 50%.

Relative Humidity is very much related to temperature. Warm air can contain a lot of invisible water vapour; cold air copes with very little.

When a parcel of air is warmed it expands so that the given amount of water vapour at the time becomes relatively less in relation to the size of the parcel. The reverse happens when the parcel is cooled.

Suffice it to say that when a parcel of air can no longer hold any more water vapour, the amount of vapour is said to have reached 100%.

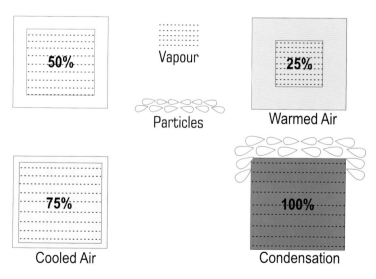

Relative Humidity

Condensation

When air is cooled to a point where the Relative Humidity reaches 100%, any further cooling will see the excess vapour change into VISIBLE water particles. The process is known as condensation – I am sure you understand this as it happens to often in ordinary life. The first sign of it taking place in the sky is a cloud forming.

You will have seen by now that although temperature and Relative Humidity are two separate items, they are closely related to each other. A thought running through your mind may be – why do these visible particles not fall to the ground? Simple – they are so minute and light at the time that they remain in the air.

When condensation takes place at ground level and the particles latch on to, say, a cold metal surface they can join together and form water droplets such as those you see on your car. Your next thought may be – why is it on my car but there is no cloud in the sky? Quite simply there may not be the amount of water vapour aloft at the time compared with the amount at the surface. I told you met can be full of foibles – hence the need of continuous observations and measurements being made all round the world both on the surface and in the air.

Before leaving the subject of visible water particles, should the temperature be below freezing point then condensed particles can actually be in the form of ice crystals.

Cloud

Measuring Relative Humidity

You may ask (in fact I was afraid you might) how Relative Humidity is measured? I don't think it would be going too far to assume that you have often seen a damp surface gradually become dry and that you know this process to be called evaporation. I also presume that you are aware that when you have washed your hair the next stage is applying the drier and in doing so have you not at times experienced a cooling effect on your head as the drier does its work? For those who have no hair, try this angle. On coming out of the sea on a hot summer's day have you not suddenly felt cold until you gradually dried out in the sun?

The lesson here is when evaporation takes place there is a temperature loss as the particles are being returned to vapour. With this fact in mind, the met man gets hold of another thermometer and covers the bulb at the bottom with cloth which is soaked by water fed to it from a reservoir below. This second thermometer, known as a wet bulb, is usually placed alongside the one already in place (dry bulb) to measure air temperature.

If the air is very dry the evaporation will be quite substantial so likewise will be the drop in temperature on the thermometer as the wet bulb cloth imparts its water back into invisible vapour. If the RH happens to be 100%, this means no evaporation will be able to take place (the air cannot take in any more vapour) so there is no cooling and the wet bulb thermometer will read the same as the dry bulb one alongside. The RH figure is obtained by comparing the dry bulb reading with the wet bulb reading using a laid down conversion table.

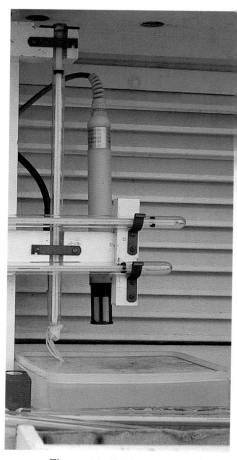

The wet bulb thermometer is the vertical one

Decrease in Temperature of Condensed Rising Air

Sorry but we're back to the good old parcel of rising air for a moment due to the effect moisture can have on it. Nature delights in events with direct opposites. The one we need to know at the moment is as follows. If you have cooling with evaporation you will have warming when the opposite (condensation) takes place.

If you have not at this stage returned to a novel instead of this humble effort, note what can happen when condensation takes place during a forced air ascent. The parcel may reach the level where its temperature is equal to its surround – where normally the ascent would come to a halt. But, should condensation take place at that moment, the warmth caused now reduces the parcel's cooling rate per 1000 feet by half 1.5°C (2.7°F). This means that the parcel instead of reaching equality remains warmer than its surround and the ascent thus continues to even higher levels.

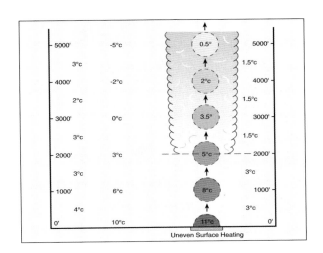

Effect of heat in cloud on a parcel's climb rate

So, what have we learnt up to now?

- *Cooling air beyond the stage where its Relative Humidity becomes 100% will cause the excess* invisible *water vapour to condense into* visible *water particles or ice crystals – namely cloud.*

- *Condensation can take place on the ground and not in the sky. It can take place in the sky and not on the ground or it can take place or not take place in both. It all depends on the water vapour content and temperature in the locations at the time.*

- *If the temperature is below freezing point the particles can be of ice.*

- *Water can join together to form larger water droplets.*

- *The rate at which temperature in the atmosphere decreases with height constantly varies.*

- *A parcel of dry air forced to rise up through the atmosphere will cool at a fixed rate of 3°C (5.4°F).*

- *After condensation has taken place the fixed rate becomes 1.5°C (2.7°F).*

- *After condensation the climb of a parcel now visible as cloud can accelerate.*

CLOUDS

Clouds are ever changing and thus fit in perfectly with that other ever changing event, the weather; later you will see how they can foretell it. At the risk of repetition, first recall how clouds can form. They do so when moist air cools to the point where it can no longer hold any more water vapour. Further cooling after that point brings condensation into visible particles. Thinking of the ways in which cooling can take place, recall how temperature decreases with height and therefore air will cool if forced to ascend. So let's go straight into the ways in which this can happen.

Already we have become aware that a parcel of air at the surface will be forced to rise on becoming warmer than the air surrounding it.

Cloud forming from warm air rising from the surface

Cloud can form from air warmed by fire at the surface

Hill cloud

Another way air ascent can occur is when it flows towards a mountain range and is forced to rise on climbing over it, thus cooling to form cloud.

The atmosphere is ever restless. Like a stream of water with a ragged bed of rocks and obstructions, the flow can be very rough; so it is with air (wind) flowing over such surfaces as hills and towns. It can be sufficiently lifted to reach a condensation point.

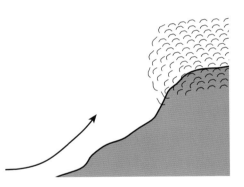

Surface causing turbulence

TURBULENCE

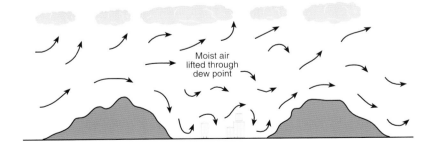

Moist air lifted through dew point

Low cloud

Turbulence can also take place far above the surface due to other factors such as temperature changes, thus causing cloud to form at a grea height without any forming lowe down.

High cloud

WAVES

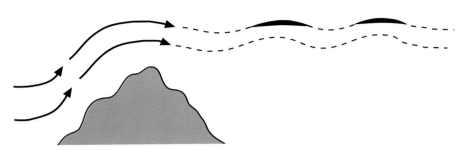

Standing wave

Mountains can cause waves in the wind that can take place far above their tops. As air cools on climbing the ascending side of the wave it can condense and form cloud only to disappear on descending after passing over the crest.

There is one other way in which air can be forced to rise; this must keep until later when you have reached the stage where it would be more readily understood.

Wave cloud

Types of cloud

Having now considered some of the ways in which clouds can form we will view the various types to be seen if you choose to look up into the sky regularly. The types are broadly classified according to the height of their base above the ground. However, the base figures can vary with the seasons, being higher in summer and lower in winter. The approximate base heights can commence from the following levels.

High   18000 feet   (5500 metres)
Medium   8000 feet   (2500 metres)
Low   Surface   + + +

We come to a situation where official met terms have to be used. Clouds have Latin names – some of which could make you fall about laughing. For example, 'Cirrus spissatus cumulonimbus genitus' is but one! Rest assured, I'll endeavour to provide you with simple interpretations as we go along.

– High cloud has the prefix 'cirro' and is so high that it is composed of ice particles

– Medium cloud has the prefix 'alto' and is composed of water particles that can at times also be of ice.

– Low cloud has no specific prefix before its type name.

Clouds with a 'cauliflower' look at the top are called 'cumuliform' – we shall call them 'cu' clouds for short. They are also sometimes called 'heap' cloud, and they form on climbing through an unstable atmosphere. Clouds in sheet form or lumps with no apparent wish to climb are known as 'stratiform' or 'layer' cloud and are associated with a stable atmosphere. Just to confuse you the 'lump' ones are also called 'cu'.

High Clouds

Cirrus

Cirro-cumulus

Cirro-stratus

Medium Clouds

Alto-cumulus

Alto-stratus

Lenticular (wave cloud)

Low Clouds
CUMILIFORM (HEAP)

Fracto not quite formed into small cu

Small cu – base is wider than height

Medium cu – height is longer than base

Large cu

Cumulonimbus or cu-nimb for short

Anvil – caused when a cu-nimb cloud stops rising and spreads out on reaching an invisible ceiling

Low Clouds
STRATIFORM (LAYER)

Stratus

Strato-cu

Fog

Fog is really no more than cloud forming at ground level. Should the relative humidity at surface level already be 100% and the air cold enough, there is no need for an ascent to be made for condensation to take place. Internationally fog is said to exist when the visibility falls below one kilometre.

Thick fog

Mist

Mist is no more than thin fog which is often the forerunner of thick fog.

Mist

Haze

Haze is not essentially a met event. The particles consist of dust trapped low down in a stable atmosphere where they are unable to be carried aloft and become dispersed.

Haze

PRECIPITATION

The word precipitation embraces all forms of water droplets and ice particles falling from clouds or forming on the ground. As mentioned earlier, in this situation the particles can be so minute and light that they float in the air and remain there. However, there comes a time when particles having moved around in cloud can join up with each other. Eventually the weight of their increased size overcomes any sustaining upward movement of air in the cloud and they fall to the ground. Bear in mind that the occurrence of precipitation and its volume, duration and extent can vary enormously according to weather system and associated clouds at the time. It will in no way happen simply because the particular cloud type is present in the sky.

Types of Precipitation

We now look at the types of precipitation in relation to the clouds from which they originate.

Rain

Type   Rain is the most common form of precipitation and can be heavy, light, continuous, intermittent or patchy according to the cloud type and its potential (temperature, relative humidity etc.) at the time.

Clouds   Nimbo-stratus, a cloud associated with continuous, sometimes heavy rain. Thick strato-cumulus can produce moderate to light or patchy rain. Large cumulus and cumulo-nimbus (cu-nimb for short) can produce moderate to heavy falls.

Note: When rain falls from isolated large cumulus or cu-nimb clouds it can be short-lived. It is referred to as a shower when lasting no more than twenty to thirty minutes at a time.

Rain shower

Hail

Type   Hail is composed of tiny stones of ice formed when water particles in cloud are carried up to a height where freezing takes place. They then descend through the cloud where they meet up with more water droplets which cling to the iced stone. The up – and down – currents can be so intense as to see the stones being repeatedly carried up and down growing larger each time. They finally fall to the ground when their weight exceeds the power of the up-currents or the up-currents gradually decrease as the cloud begins to decay.

Clouds   Intensely powerful cu-nimb.

Snow

Type   Snow occurs when condensation takes place below freezing point and ice particles are produced instead of water particles. These particles, like rain, can join together and fall as beautifully patterned crystals.

Clouds   The same as for rain or showers, but notice the slightly different colour.

Snow shower

Sleet

Type When the fall is a mixture of both rain and snow we have sleet. As snow falls it can pass through warmer air on the way down and some of the ice crystals melt into water droplets (rain).

Clouds The same as for rain or showers.

Earlier we talked of extremes. In the case of rain it is amazing how cloud climbing a range of mountains can cause incredible rainfall on its windward side but next to nothing on the other (lee) side. Take a look at the average rainfall situation in Burma on the coast compared with inland on the other side of the Chin Hills and the Arakan Yoma – I can vouch for it,

having personally collected 12.4 inches of rain in one day during the monsoon at Akyab!

In fact to the north in India is the place with the highest rainfall in the world. At Cherrapunji in the hills of Assam the Indian monsoon provides around 425 inches (10,800 millimetres) of water a year.

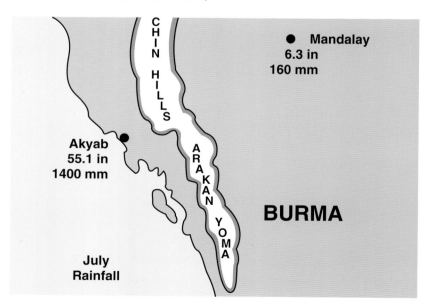

Burma rainfall

Drizzle

Type   Drizzle is actually rain but the particles are so small and light that it is officially distinguished from rain by the fact it does not make a splash when falling into a puddle.

Clouds   Thin strato-cumulus, thick stratus.

Thick stratus

Precipitation on the ground

Dew

We will return for one moment to radiation of heat from the ground. At night there will be no sun to replenish the earth's heat until it rises again the next day. As a result, the surface becomes gradually colder to the extent that condensation can take place and water particles appear on the grass and of course on the car as seen earlier.

Incidentally, there can come a time when radiation has given away so much warmth that the air immediately close to the surface becomes colder than the warm air above. Here is the situation referred to earlier where temperature can sometimes not decrease but in fact increase with height to a point.

Frost

When the same process for dew takes place, but the temperature is below freezing point, the deposit will be ice particles not water droplets. This is frost.

Frost

Black ice

This is known as black ice because unlike other ice it isn't white! In fact it isn't even black because it is invisible. It occurs when rain (not snow) falls onto frozen ground where it spreads out and freezes to form a clear film of ice which is actually deadly on pavements and roads as it can give the appearance of being only a wet surface.

AIR MASSES

Before entering the realms of air masses and weather systems with their various foibles, a quick look into the atmosphere will be useful – embracing the world pattern of pressure and temperature regions which can broadly be dubbed source points for weather.

The earth can be divided into very broad areas of high/low pressure and temperature. As discussed earlier, winds move from high to low pressure again with deflected movement due the earth's rotation.

Such winds are known as the prevailing winds because they are the ones normally experienced (or are supposed to be) in the regions over which they blow. They have an effect on air masses.

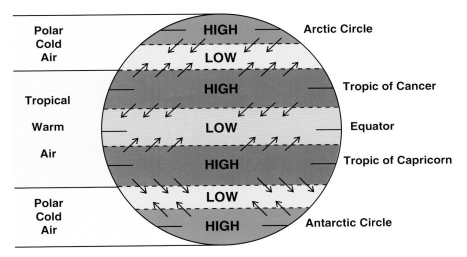

A broad picture of the world's pressure patterns and temperature regions.

The air masses referred to in the chapter title are masses of air which take on the characteristics of the area over which they normally stagnate for a length of time.

Air over the tropics will be warm and if over an ocean it will also be very moist in view of the substantial amount of water available to be evaporated into it. Air that is over land would be relatively dry with little water present to be absorbed other than from lakes and rivers. Likewise over the polar regions the air will be cold and either moist or dry according to the terrain over which it is located.

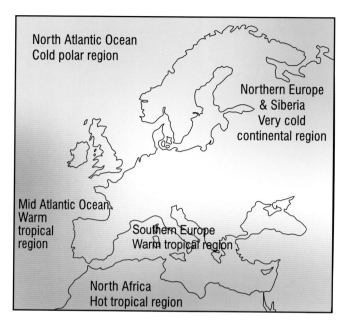

Air mass distribution

From time to time, however, due to the individual pressure systems forming, the air from a given mass can travel as an airstream to another region thus contributing to the changes in weather that can occur.

The best example of airstreams in relation to the effect they have on weather is to be found in the Northern Hemisphere where the British Isles are located in a 'pig in the middle' situation of a temperate zone between the Tropical and Polar regions.

These airstreams have official names; for simplicity we will call them the following according to their source region:

- From Polar region over the North Atlantic Ocean	*Cold and Wet*
- From Tropical region over the Mid Atlantic Ocean	*Warm and Wet*
- From Polar region over Northern Europe and Siberia	*Cold and Dry*
- From Tropical region over Southern Europe & North Africa (Sahara Desert)	*Warm and Dry*

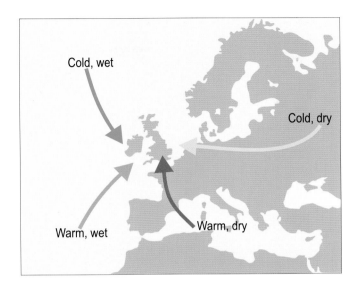

Airstream paths from source air masses

In huge continents such as North America an airstream can travel a very long way from north to south with a marked effect. It is the flow of cold air from the north meeting up with warm wet air from the Gulf of Mexico that triggers thunderstorms and tornadoes.

Some years ago I recall being very excited at leaving the UK in the month of March for the warmth of Florida. In fact the temperature turned out to be 17 degrees Fahrenheit below normal for the few days I was there – all due to a flow of cold air from the North!

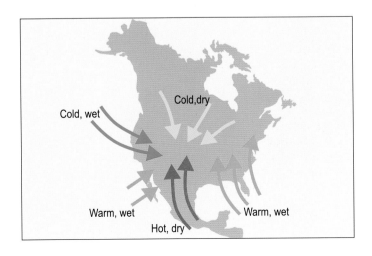

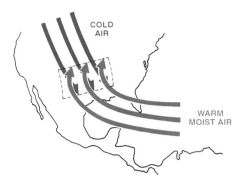

America

Again in America where cold air from the north sweeps down to meet very warm moist air flowing in from the Gulf of Mexico, the result is usually heavy rain-hail from thunderstorms plus the possibility of tornadoes.

The flow of such airstreams can indeed have a large bearing on the type of weather – also the border line where differing air masses meet can have the same effect as you will see in the later chapter on fronts.

Each year in the Far East, Asia, the continent containing India, Burma and other lands close at hand all experience months of rain. Due to the intensely hot air rising over this landmass the cooler/moist air flows in from the Indian Ocean onto the land and the monsoon commences.

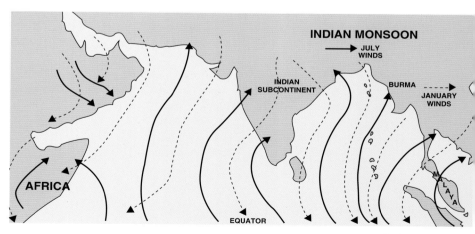

Indian monsoon

WEATHER

Weather is closely related to pressure systems (and of course, subsequent airstreams) – recall how earlier it was mentioned that most of the simple home-type barometers have types of weather on their faces. One of these instruments is well worth having, to be warned of weather changes before they appear in your locality. There are four systems you need bother about.

To put you completely in the picture, in met terms the high pressure centre is usually known as a 'high' but officially it is called an 'anti-cyclone'. The low pressure centre is usually known as a 'low' but is officially called a 'depression' – very apt as its weather is always depressing! How they form can be complicated enough but when they form is left to a 'power from above'.

Depression

Let's talk about 'old misery guts' first. Perhaps one way of explaining its formation is that air in the upper regions of the atmosphere can suddenly increase in speed and before the air behind it can catch up you can have a sort of 'gap' where temporarily there is relatively less air.

Remember when we talked about two glasses of water joined together? In this case, as Nature endeavours to equalise things, apart from a horizontal flow we would now have a vertical flow as the air from the surface ascends to fill the 'gap' taking place above. In this case it does so very gradually and in no way as fast as even the lightest wind. The result of the rising air is a decrease of pressure at the surface, thus producing a 'low' as we shall call it.

Next remember when we talked about what happens to rising air? It cools, does it not? And, if it is moist enough, it can condense into water particles which eventually could grow into water droplets big enough to fall to Mother Earth.

Well with practically all lows this is just what happens. A low is therefore very much associated with bad weather capable of continuous rain/sleet/snow and high winds when it is known to be deep (or intense), that is, the isobars are close together. How long it will affect you depends entirely on how fast the centre is travelling and where you are located in relation to it. Sometimes it can be stationary which is not helpful if it is directly above you.

How do we know one is coming? The obvious answer is when a barometer is indicating a positive decline in pressure.

FORMATION OF A DEPRESSION

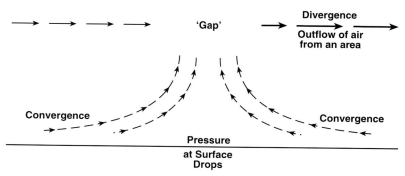

Divergence and convergence

Trough

The trough, as the name implies, can produce a 'pig of a day' with the same sort of weather as its 'parent' low, except that being only a tongue it can pass over you more rapidly.

Anti-cyclone

Here we come to 'sweetness and light' – but not always. Being a 'high' it is the reverse of a 'low', which means it has air descending and increasing pressure at the surface. Again the reverse is happening so that instead of the air cooling on ascent, this air warms on descent and will then be capable of holding much more water vapour. The result is relatively little or no condensation taking place and therefore there can be little or no rain.

Here at times you can experience glorious summer weather with endless sunshine in a cloudless sky but plenty of haze reducing visibility. The magnitude of its favours depends entirely on its size, strength, and how fast it is moving in relation to you.

The winds are usually light but having said that, they can be quite steady and strong around the outer extremities.

In winter, this system can paint a very different picture. The cold air is much closer to condensation point than in summer and fog is quite on the cards – almost certainly in the late afternoon to early morning from late autumn to spring. As fog likes virtually calm weather the likelihood is even greater. If the sun should conjure up enough warmth the fog can be lifted to become low stratus cloud which, when it is forming a blanket totally covering the sky, produces a miserable but dry situation called 'anti-cyclonic gloom'.

How do we know an anti-cyclone is coming? Once again the answer is when a barometer is indicating a positive increase in pressure.

Anti-cyclone

Ridge

Similar to a trough, but this time being a tongue of high pressure, a ridge can produce anti-cyclonic weather but it will naturally not last as long as its 'parent' high. Also, you are unlikely to experience those dead calm spells that can come with the said 'parent' but you could be free from the winter fog or 'gloom' mentioned above. The ridge is usually a break between two frontal systems. Frontal systems play a major part in weather and are explained in the following chapter.

Violent Weather

Thunderstorms

When ice particles in a cu-nimb cloud join together to form hailstones, as they rage up and down in the strong currents within this type of cloud an electrical charge is created which, when it becomes intensely powerful, breaks away to find earth (the electrical one). This break-away is called lightning and can be in two forms.

When its target is the ground it will be visible in a zig-zag pattern known as fork lightning. Should the target happen to be within another cu-nimb close by it will not been seen as a zig-zag as it travels within the clouds from one to the other. It will vividly illuminate them, whereupon it is called sheet lightning. The frightening clap of thunder associated with the lightning is caused by what can best be described as the explosion that comes about due to the effect of the lightning's intense heat on the immediate surrounding air.

Lightning path

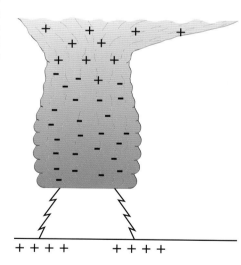

How do we know a thunderstorm is coming? The short answer to this is the appearance of cu-nimb clouds and a hot sticky unstable atmosphere – hence so many thunderstorms occur in the tropical regions. In the temperate zone during summer they are most likely to occur when a high, which has given you such lovely weather over a week or even more, begins to break down – a barometer check will tell you this before the sky does so.

In the above situation, a thunderstorm needs an unstable atmosphere – where air can shoot rapidly from the surface into the upper air. But there can be the situation where the stable atmosphere associated with the declining high will have been great for trapping haze near the surface and therefore you may not initially notice the gradual build up of cu-nimb clouds in the distance at first – the visibility being poor due to the haze. A distant rumble might be the first hint you get. When it finally reaches you, make no mistake, the sky will be very different to what it has been in previous days.

Cu-nimb – the source of the thunderstorm

Thunderstorm approaching

There is another cloud type that gives an indication of potential thundery conditions being triggered off at medium level. It has the name of 'alto-cumulus' and forms in a stable atmosphere, but when the suffix 'cas' is added (real name 'castellanus') it means that medium level instability is developing. There are two interesting foibles about alto-cu cas (Ac cas).

First, when it appears in the sky it does not mean that a thunderstorm will necessarily develop at that location but usually one will occur within a hundred-mile radius. Second, it used to be called 'castellatus'. For years I used this name until reprimanded one day. It appears that unknown to me the name had changed; on asking why I was told 'someone must have done it but no one knows whom'!

One way or another, thunderstorms are not pleasant but for those who cannot bear a heat wave they are a blessing. Now to some of the extremes in weather.

Alto-cu cas – thunderstorm 72 miles (116 km) away

The Hurricane

The hurricane is a vicious brute born off the West African coast from thunderstorms grouping together to form a very deep intense depression. It moves across the Atlantic Ocean, usually ending up in the Caribbean and the southern regions of America.

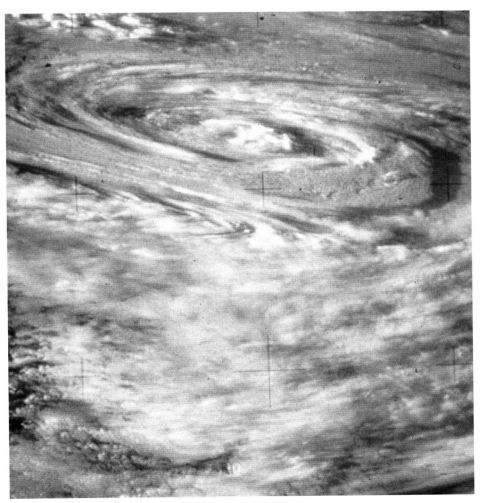

Hurricane

The Tornado

A tornado is even more vicious than a hurricane but influences a relatively small area compared with the former. The big ones mostly occur in the southern part of America but many other countries in the world are also affected by them. Again it is in a sense an extremely intense type of depression — just as wind flows around a depression so the wind around the tornado does the same but at unbelievable speeds with its spiral sucking up any loose objects in its way or destroying some firmly fixed to the ground. The damage can be horrendous.

Tornado

Wall cloud – can indicate signs of a tornado

FRONTAL SYSTEMS

Fronts

You have probably seen or heard the term 'front' on TV, computer or radio and no doubt you already associate it with bad weather. To understand the nature of a front is not difficult; it is simply the meeting line where warm air meets cold air or vice versa. They are depicted by the 'triangles' and 'mole-hills' mentioned at the beginning of this book.

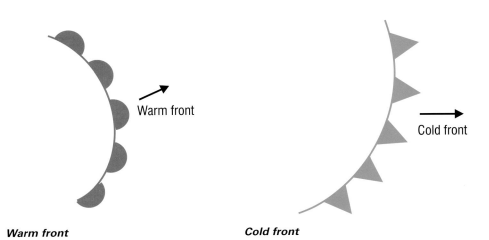

Warm front

Warm front

Cold front

Cold front

The term front originates from the name given to the battle zones in World War One – as warm and cold air clash there is usually a weather battle. Why is this so? Warm air moving towards cold air, by being warmer is less dense and therefore lighter. So, as they clash, being unable to penetrate the heavier (more dense) cold air it climbs over it. Cold air moving towards warm air is heavier (more dense) and will undercut the warm air (less dense), lifting it away from the surface.

Earlier when we explored the ways in which air can be forced to rise you were told that there was a fifth way to come later. Well, here it is. It is called 'frontal'. You will recall that when air is forced to rise the result can be condensation eventually resulting in precipitation and associated misery.

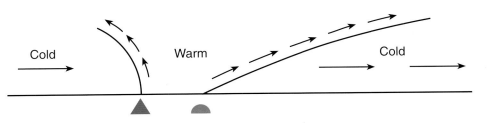

Side view of frontal system

Polar depression fronts

Polar depression fronts are well known in the temperate zones – the zones where warm tropical air meets cold polar air. Unlike other fronts, the polar ones, are invariably associated with depressions which broadly move from east to west.

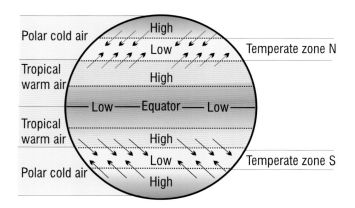

Temperate zones

Bad weather on the way

The chapter Air Masses showed the paths of airstreams from the various air masses. Two of these airstreams are cold wet air moving south and warm wet air moving north. Their meeting point is broadly defined by our old friends the mole-hills and triangles alternating along a line – a form of stationary front representing the location where the two airstreams meet at which point nature is uncertain what to do at the time!

Cold

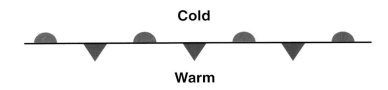

Warm

Stationary front

So, what can happen to cause a possible battle along this peaceful line? Well, every now and then nature stirs and a kink develops in the line – usually in the North Atlantic off the American-Canadian coast in the Northern Hemisphere. The fronts then begin to develop.

Cold

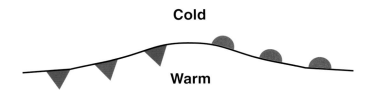

Warm

The kink

Frontal development

As the system develops the 'kink' becomes an increasing wedge of tropical warm air intruding into the polar cold air and a low begins to form around it. Here you have your frontal system specifically related to a low and moving east with it – the normal pattern of frontal systems found in temperate zones.

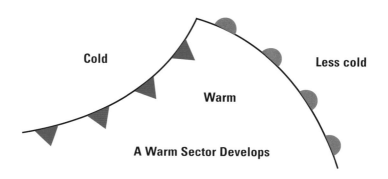

Cold

Less cold

Warm

A Warm Sector Develops

Development of a frontal system from above

Eventually all the warm air will have been lifted from the surface by the overtaking cold front so that there is no longer warm sector on the surface. This development is called an occlusion. Since an occlusion occurs as this type of frontal system is declining I am quite happy if you think of it as a 'conclusion'!

Occlusion – side view

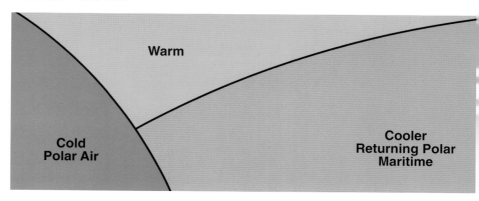

Warm

Cold
Polar Air

Cooler
Returning Polar
Maritime

Here we come to the alternating 'mole-hill' and 'triangle' set-up that you can see on the TV map and possibly in some newspapers. It can start to bend back round the depression looking rather like a scorpion's tail as it does so. It can then start to plonk rain down on an area that thought it was all over.

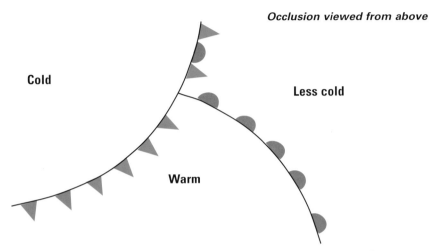

Occlusion viewed from above

Cold air overtakes and undercuts the warm to form an occlusion

Finally, the mature frontal system looks as follows.

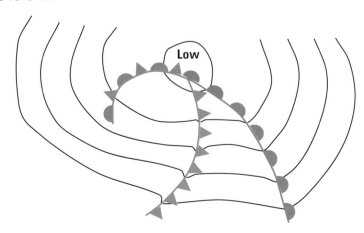

A mature polar depression frontal system

Frontal clouds and related weather

As fronts spend a substantial amount of time forcing air to rise you should now be able to deduce that a lot of cloud will be present and as clouds play an enormous part in weather conditions you can imagine the significant effect fronts can have on such conditions. How do we know one is coming? Apart from the barometer pressure dropping due to any depression associated with the temperate zone system, the clouds are a good indication. Here is a cloud and weather sequence of such a typical frontal system.

1. First there will be the appearance in the western sky of cirrus increasing and thickening into cirro-stratus.

Cirro-stratus

2. The cirro-stratus will thicken and lower to become alto-stratus. As the alto-stratus in turn thickens and lowers in height rain can begin to fall but initially it can evaporate before reaching the ground.

Cirro-stratus/alto-stratus

3. The alto-stratus continues to thicken and descend until rain begins to reach the ground. The alto-stratus will continue to descend yet further down until it is really in the low cloud category. At this stage all shape of the cloud will be lost in continuous heavy rain, which is when the thick alto-stratus lowering to low cloud level becomes nimbo-stratus.

Nimbo-stratus

4. As the warm front passes though, a veer in the wind can be noticed and the rain eases off or perhaps ceases all together. The sky becomes relatively brighter with the cloud becoming a mixture of stratus and strato-cumulus. Any rain is likely to be slight or patchy.

5. You are now in what is known as the warm sector and you may notice the change to a warmer temperature.

6. As the cold front approaches, the sky darkens once more and another period of nimbo-stratus provides more continuous rain. This period of continuous rain does not last as long as the first.

7. As the front passes by the wind veers again and finally the sky brightens up and blue skies appear with a distinct line of cirrus high cloud depicting the departing frontal system.

Departure of ana cold front

Departure of unstable ana cold front

8. There are occasions when the cold front can be composed of unstable air in which case as it passes through there will be a shorter but sharper downpour than there would be from nimbo-stratus. There can even be thunder from the cu-nimb clouds which develop and love to revel in unstable air.

9. As the cold front passes you are now in what is known as the cold sector where again you may detect the drop in temperature. The sky will appear clear for a time but soon large cumulus and even cu-nimb can build up with the possibility of heavy shower activity. (See page 84.)

The 'conclusion' (occlusion), should one form, can play nasty tricks if the air within it is still being lifted, cooled and capable of producing precipitation. Should this be the case the rain will re-commence similar to that experienced with the warm front. Should it be dying out then it would normally appear as medium cloud.

It must be understood that fronts can be weak or vigorous and it can be quite a task trying to assess a front's potential from the clouds that initially come into sight. This is where apart from using your eyes you must also check weather forecasts – the strength is usually hinted at when the forecaster refers to the likely rain being either heavy or patchy.

Again the use of eyes is important when a frontal system is forecast to be upon you at a given time. It may be that when that time comes it can either be but a faint sign in the distance to the west or you have been drenched already for the past hour or so! Fronts can speed up or slow down to a certain extent – this where the visual can be very useful. Also, if your barometer has not started to fall then the front has yet to reach you.

The cold sector

WEATHER REPORTING

It is worth having a brief look into the regular weather reporting touched upon in the chapter Pressure. A report is compiled from observations made usually on the hour throughout the day and night. They are fed to a centre which interchanges such observations with other centres, with the result that every country in the world is aware of the current global situation at that hour. Such reports will be made up broadly in a code form covering the following factors.

Pressure

The atmospheric pressure at the time adjusted to read as if at sea level.

Temperature

The dry and wet bulb temperatures whilst screened from direct sun and wind.

Pressure Tendency

Whether the pressure is rising or falling.

Screen

Rain gauge

Precipitation

The amount of rain deposited in the period. The amount of snow in depth.

Sunshine

The hours of sunshine scorched onto a chart by a magnifying glass.

Sunshine recorder

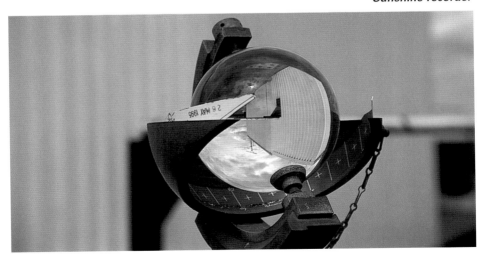

Wind

The wind speed and direction are measured by anemometers and wind vanes (pictured earlier in the book).

Visibility

The lowest distance visible at the time.

Visibility meter

Clouds

The base of clouds present and their amount in relation to the total sky. (Personal observation)

Present weather

Rain, snow, showers, fog, thunderstorms, etc. (Personal observation)

Past weather

A reminder of the previous report.

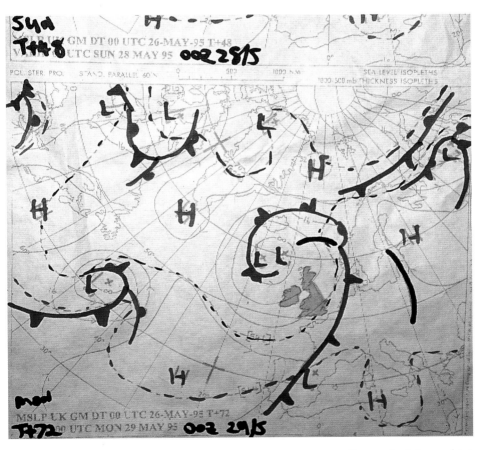

Forecaster's base chart

THE FUTURE

With *The Vital Guide to Weather* you have now had a glimpse into the realm of meteorology – hopefully it was devoid of jargon as promised and with many of the explanations being as close as possible to everyday experience you can come across. Perhaps you may wish to go a further step? I did and have never regretted it. My fascination for the sky started as a met observer in World War Two while producing continuous ground reports. The reports from all the other stations came through on a tele-printer, and as this was before the days of computers it meant poring over a chart with two pens (one blue and one red) tied together with an elastic band. Ultimately, with my help they would produce all the reports as a picture for the duty 'sacred god' – the forecaster. This was the great position I never reached – at the time lacking those impressive letters after your name that are only available from a university!

Later in the Far East, where in wartime, reporting stations were few and far between, it meant flying along intended routes to see what conditions were like before the rest set off. In tropical weather this could be most 'stimulating' (frightening) as in that part of the world clouds such as the cu-nimb extend to a far greater height and their power is much greater – capable of breaking up quite large aircraft at times.

I became hooked on met for two reasons. First, as an ordinary member of the public I found the sky was fantastic in its ability be a picture of sheer beauty one minute only to wreak terrible consequences not long afterwards. It was impossible after such involvement not to be continually watching the sky in an attempt to assess what was on the way. For years it has paid off in deciding successfully whether, say, to take the family for a picnic or not; should it be on a mountain, a valley or at the coast. This is simply by being able to make a reasonable assessment of these TV forecasts. (Yes, indeed, the foibles of met have led me to make some 'cock-ups' in so doing. You learn to take the stick after a time.)

The second reason was becoming involved in recreational flying. With gliding I soon realised on becoming a pilot (and later an instructor) that, with no engine and reliance on seeking out invisible up-currents in the air, met became a must. Indeed, it is well known that the experienced glider pilot eventually becomes an experienced meteorologist – necessary when travelling a long distance with no engine. With powered aeroplanes the particular knowledge needed by the glider pilot to remain airborne is not needed. This can result in the pilots not being sufficiently 'met-ised'! In fact without doubt it is another 'must' in that the weather can present many dangers. It can be an eye-opener at times when flying with other pilots alleged to be 'seasoned' but heading into trouble.

The two reasons have led to a desire to share my non-professional knowledge of the subject with both public and pilot after many years accumulating pictures of sky and weather systems. I have done so in the form of two books – both crammed with colour pictures – and, although adopting the 'KISS' philosophy, they go just that much deeper and cover a broader spectrum. Call it a 'commercial' if you like but, after *The Vital Guide to Weather*, if you wish to delve further into this capricious but fascinating subject then here is one of two books awaiting you: *The World of Weather*. This book is for those who wish to make more of the media forecasts to plan their weekends off with the family, the prospects for that important match or their children's desire to pass that all-important exam. But also you will learn more about hurricanes, tornadoes and suchlike activities in other parts of the world.

Pilot's Weather is aimed at the student pilot but is equally important for many qualified pilots (as some have already admitted). It not only covers the theory on what the weather is, needed by the student for the licence exam, but also what the weather *can do* to both aeroplane and pilot – a crucial issue perhaps not given the thought it deserves at times.

INDEX

air, moisture in   31–6
air and temperature   25–30
air masses   60–64
airstreams   62–63, 64, 76
anti-cyclone (high pressure centre)
    65, 67
atmospheric conditions, stable and
    unstable   29, 30

barometers   9, 10, 11, 65, 66, 67

clouds   33, 36, 37–52, 54
    frontal   80–84
    reporting   89
    types   42–9
        high   40, 42, 43, 44, 80–81
        low (cumuliform – cu; heap)   40,
        42, 46–8, 68, 69, 81, 82, 83, 90
        low (stratiform; layer)   42, 49, 67
        medium   41, 42, 44, 45, 70, 81
cold sector   83, 84
condensation   33, 35, 36, 37, 66, 75

daylight, hours   22
depression (low pressure centre)   65, 66
dew   58
drizzle   57

earth, heat radiating   21, 23, 24, 30, 58
evaporation   34

flying   91
fog   50, 66
fronts (frontal systems)   74–77, 79, 82,
    83
    cloud and weather sequence   80–83
    development   78
frost   59

hail   54
haze   52, 69
heat, source of   21–4 see also
    temperature
heat loss on ascent   26–30, 36
heat radiating from sea   23, 24, 30
humidity, relative (RH)   32, 33, 34, 36,
    50
hurricanes   71

ice   33, 36, 59
isobars   13, 16, 17

'kink'   77, 78

lightning   68

mist   51
moisture in the air   31–6
monsoons   56, 64
mountains   41

occlusion   78–9, 83

precipitation   53–9, 87
pressure   8–13
    centres   13, 17, 18, 65, 66, 67
    pattern, world   61
    reporting   86
    system, airflow around   17
    units of measurement   12, 17

rain   54, 56, 87
'ridge'   13, 68

screen   86
sleet   56
snow   55
sun, position of   5, 21–2
sunshine, reporting   87
surface heating characteristics   23, 24,
    30

temperate zones   76
temperature   19–30 see also heat,
    source of
    and the air   25–30
    conversion   20
    loss on ascent   26, 29, 30, 35, 36
    measurement   19–20
    reporting   86
    world regions   61
thermometers   20, 34
thunderstorms   68–70
tornadoes   64, 72–3
'trough'   13, 67
turbulence   39, 40

visibility, reporting   88

warm sector   83
wave, standing   41
weather   65–73
    maps, TV   3–4
    reporting   85–89
    violent   68–73
wind   14–18, 61, 87

92